I Meet Listening

3

Happy House

CONTENTS

Syllabus

Unit	Theme	Title
Unit 01	Clothes	**What Are You Wearing?**
Unit 02	Price	**How Much Is This?**
Unit 03	Place	**I'm Going to the Park**
Unit 04	Job ①	**I Want to Be a Teacher**
Unit 05	Job ②	**Why Do You Want to Be a Teacher?**

Review Test I (Units 01-05)

Unit	Theme	Title
Unit 06	Transportation	**You Can Get There by Train**
Unit 07	Seasons & Activities	**I Go Swimming**
Unit 08	Holiday	**When Is Christmas?**
Unit 09	Subject	**What Is Your Favorite Subject?**
Unit 10	School Rules	**Sit Down, Please**

Review Test II (Units 06-10)

Words	Key Listening
shirt, pants, skirt, jacket, dress, shoes	What are you wearing? I'm wearing a shirt and pants.
twenty-five cents, fifty cents, one dollar, one dollar and fifty cents, six dollars and forty cents, ten dollars	How much is this? It's fifty cents.
theater, school, bank, mall, park, pet shop	Where are you going? I'm going to the park.
firefighter, doctor, teacher, cook, pilot, artist	What do you want to be? I want to be a teacher.
teach kids, help sick people, save people, make food, fly planes, paint pictures	Why do you want to be a teacher? Because I want to teach kids.

Words	Key Listening
on foot, by bus, by car, by subway, by train, by airplane	How can I get there? You can get there by train.
spring, summer, fall, winter, go hiking, go swimming, go camping, go skiing	What do you do in summer? I go swimming.
Christmas, Halloween, New Year's Day, Valentine's Day, December 25, October 31, January 1, February 14	When Is Christmas? Christmas is on December 25.
English, science, math, art, music, P.E.	What is your favorite subject? My favorite subject is music.
sit, quiet, stand, run, fight, late	Sit down, please. Okay, I will sit down.

What Are You Wearing?

Fun Listening

Listen to the cartoon. Then put on the stickers. CD 1 02 Page 81

Listen, point, and say. CD 1 03

Clothes

shirt   pants   skirt   jacket   dress   shoes

A Listen, match, and say. CD 1 04

1 

2 

3

4

5

6

• pants •
• dress •
• shirt •
• jacket •
• skirt •
• shoes •

B Listen and circle. CD 1 05

1  

2  

3 

4

A Listen, match, and say. CD 1 06

1 

2 

3 

- I'm wearing shoes.

- I'm wearing a jacket.

- I'm wearing a dress.

B Listen and check. CD 1 07

1 

2 

3 

4 

A Listen and repeat. Then practice. CD 1 08

B Listen, choose, and write. CD 1 09

1

Q What are you wearing?

A I'm wearing _____________.

ⓐ shoes　　ⓑ a skirt　　ⓒ pants

2

Q What are you wearing?

A I'm wearing _____________.

ⓐ a jacket　　ⓑ pants　　ⓒ a shirt

C Listen and number. CD 1 10

A Listen and write. (CD 1 · 11)

It's Time for a Play!

They have a play today.
Mark is wearing a big ___________.
Nancy is wearing a dress and shoes.
Jim is ___________ a shirt and pants.
They look great!

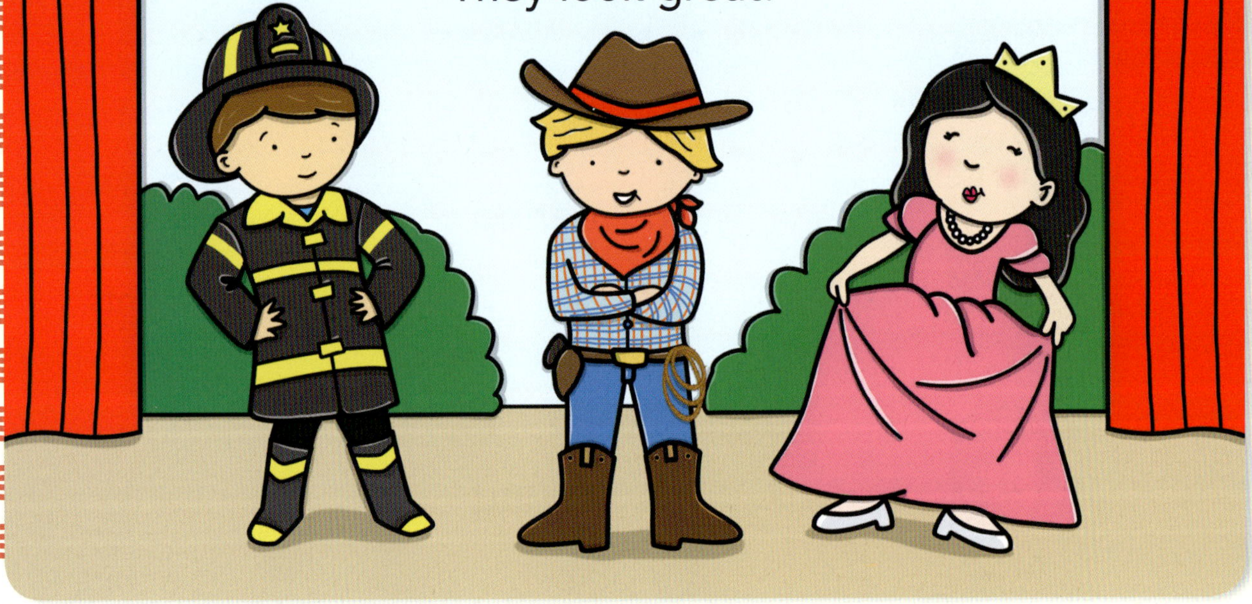

Hint Box
wearing
jacket

B Read and choose.

1 What is Mark wearing?

   ⓐ a big jacket   ⓑ a dress   ⓒ a skirt

2 How do they look?

   ⓐ funny   ⓑ not good   ⓒ great

Ask and listen. Then write. 

What are you wearing?

Teacher

I'm wearing _______________.

Friend 1

I'm wearing _______________.

Friend 2

I'm wearing _______________.

Draw your clothes. Then talk to your class.

I'm wearing _______________.

How Much Is This?

Fun Listening

Listen to the cartoon. Then put on the stickers. CD 1 12 — Page 81

Listen, point, and say. CD 1 13

A Listen, match, and say. (CD 1 / 14)

1

2

- one dollar -

- six dollars and forty cents -

- ten dollars -

- fifty cents -

- one dollar and fifty cents -

- twenty-five cents -

3

4

5
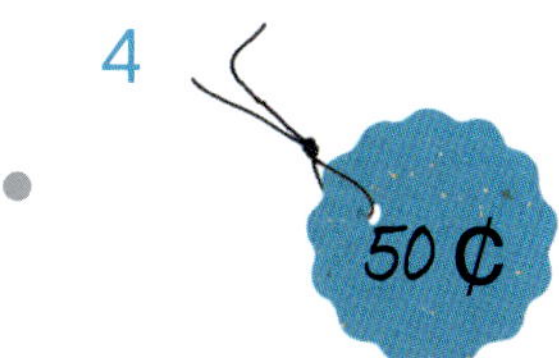

6

B Listen and number. (CD 1 / 15)

A Listen, match, and say. (CD 1 / 16)

1 

•   • It's fifty cents.

2 

•   • It's ten dollars.

3 

•   • It's one dollar and fifty cents.

B Listen and check. (CD 1 / 17)

1 

2 

3 

4 

A Listen and repeat. Then practice. CD 1 · 18

B Listen, choose, and write. CD 1 · 19

1

Q How much is this?

A It's _______________________ .

(a) twenty-five cents   (b) fifty cents

2

Q How much is this?

A It's _______________________ .

(a) one dollar and fifty cents   (b) ten dollars

C Listen and number. CD 1 · 20

John Can't Buy It

Jane asks, "How much is this cup?"
The woman says, "It's _________."
John asks, "How _________ is this T-shirt?"
The woman says, "It's $6.40."
John only has $5. He can't buy it.

B **Read and choose.**

1 How much is the cup?

   ⓐ 50¢   ⓑ $1.50   ⓒ $6.40

2 What does John want to buy?

   ⓐ pants   ⓑ a T-shirt   ⓒ shoes

Ask and listen. Then write. 

HOW much is your shirt?

Teacher
It's ____________________.

Friend 1
It's ____________________.

Friend 2
It's ____________________.

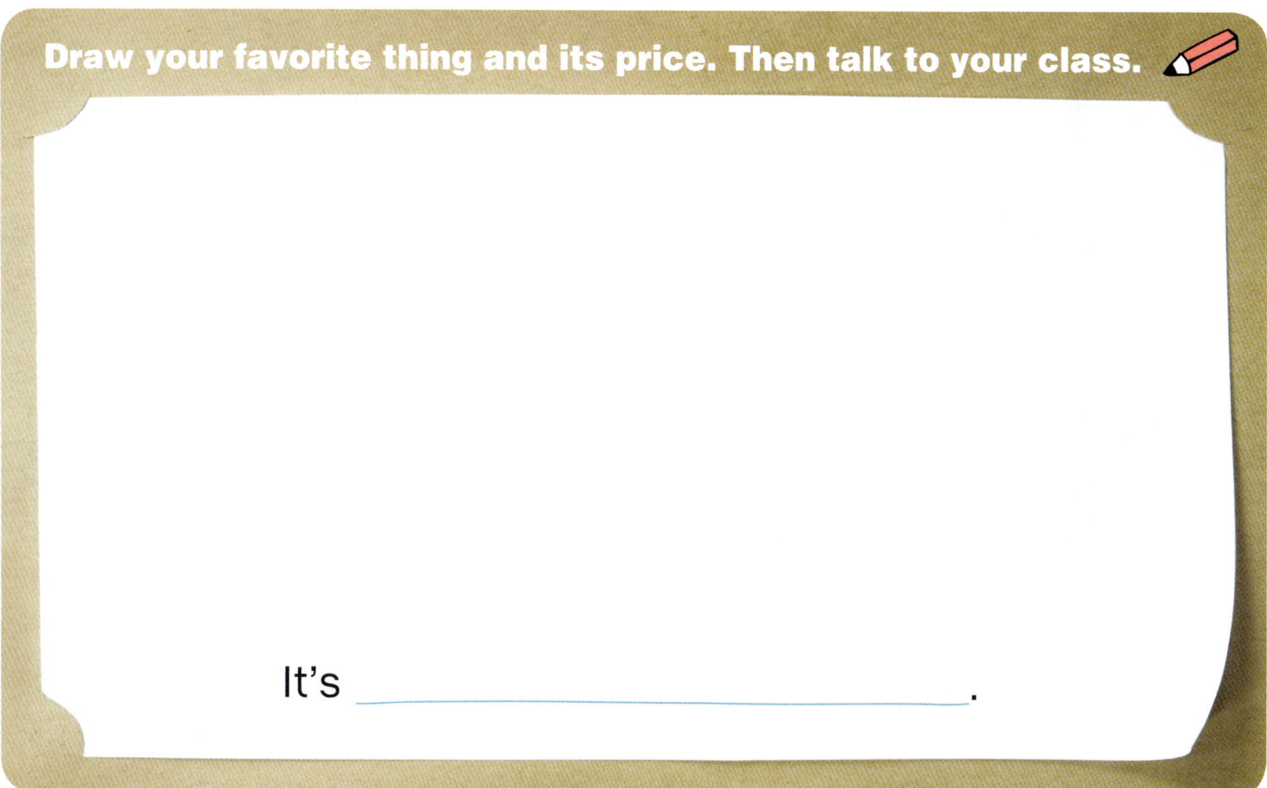

I'm Going to the Park

Listen to the cartoon. Then put on the stickers. CD 1 22 · Page 81

Listen, point, and say. CD 1 23

Place

 theater

 school

 bank

 mall

 park

 pet shop

A Listen, circle, and say. 🎧 CD 1 24

1

theater | park

2

bank | pet shop

3

mall | school

4

pet shop | mall

5

park | theater

6

bank | school

B Listen and number. 🎧 CD 1 25

A Listen, check, and say. CD 1 26

1 
- ◯ I'm going to the park.
- ◯ I'm going to the pet shop.

2 
- ◯ I'm going to the mall.
- ◯ I'm going to the theater.

3 
- ◯ I'm going to school.
- ◯ I'm going to the bank.

B Listen and circle. CD 1 27

1 

2 

3 

4 

A Listen and repeat. Then practice. CD 1 28

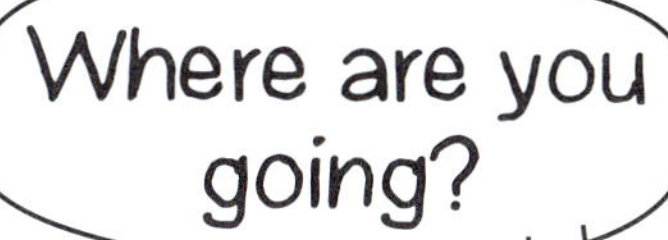

school
the park
the theater

B Listen, choose, and write. CD 1 29

1

Q Where are you going?

A I'm going to the _______________.

ⓐ theater　　ⓑ pet shop　　ⓒ mall

2

Q Where are you going?

A I'm going to the _______________.

ⓐ park　　ⓑ theater　　ⓒ bank

C Listen and number. CD 1 30

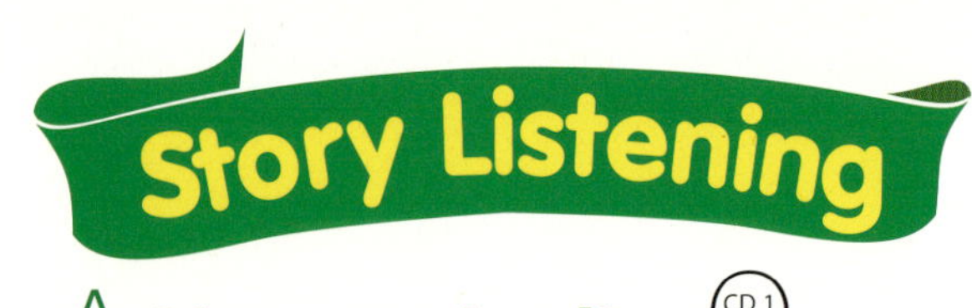

Story Listening

A Listen and write. CD 1 31

Where Are You Going?

Hint Box
Where
school

Linda meets Tom and Kate in the park.
Tom is going to ________.
Kate is going to the theater.
"________ are you going, Linda?" they ask.
"Oops! I'm going to the pet shop!" says Linda.

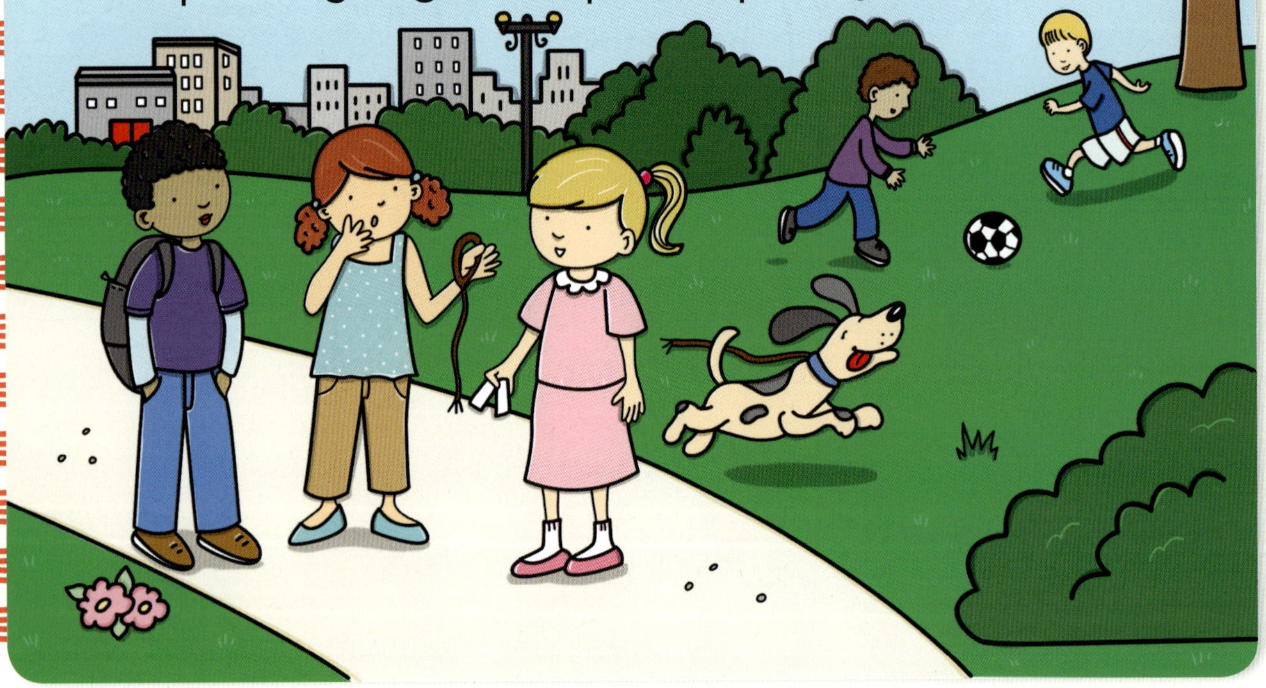

B Read and choose.

1 Where is Kate going?

ⓐ to the theater ⓑ to school ⓒ to the pet shop

2 Where is Linda going?

ⓐ to the park ⓑ to the pet shop ⓒ to school

Ask and answer. Then write. 

Where are you going?

Draw your favorite place. Then talk to your class.

I'm going to the ________________.

Fun Listening

Listen to the cartoon. Then put on the stickers.  CD 1 32 Page 81

Listen, point, and say. CD 1 33

Job ❶

Word Listening

A Listen, circle, and say. CD 1 34

1 doctor | teacher

2 artist | firefighter

3 teacher | cook

4 cook | artist

5 firefighter | pilot

6 cook | doctor

B Listen and circle. CD 1 35

1

2

3

4

A Listen, check, and say. (CD 1 · 36)

1

○ I want to be a teacher.

○ I want to be an artist.

2

○ I want to be a pilot.

○ I want to be a cook.

3

○ I want to be a doctor.

○ I want to be a firefighter.

B Listen and check. (CD 1 · 37)

1

2

3

4

A Listen and repeat. Then practice. CD 1 38

B Listen, choose, and write. CD 1 39

1

Q What do you want to be?

A I want to be _______________.

ⓐ a pilot   ⓑ a doctor   ⓒ an artist

2

Q What do you want to be?

A I want to be _______________.

ⓐ a firefighter   ⓑ a cook   ⓒ a teacher

C Listen and number. CD 1 40

A Listen and write. CD 1 41

Show and Tell

Our class is talking about jobs.
Sam wants to be a __________.
Jack wants to be an artist.
Judy __________ to be a doctor.
What do you want to be?

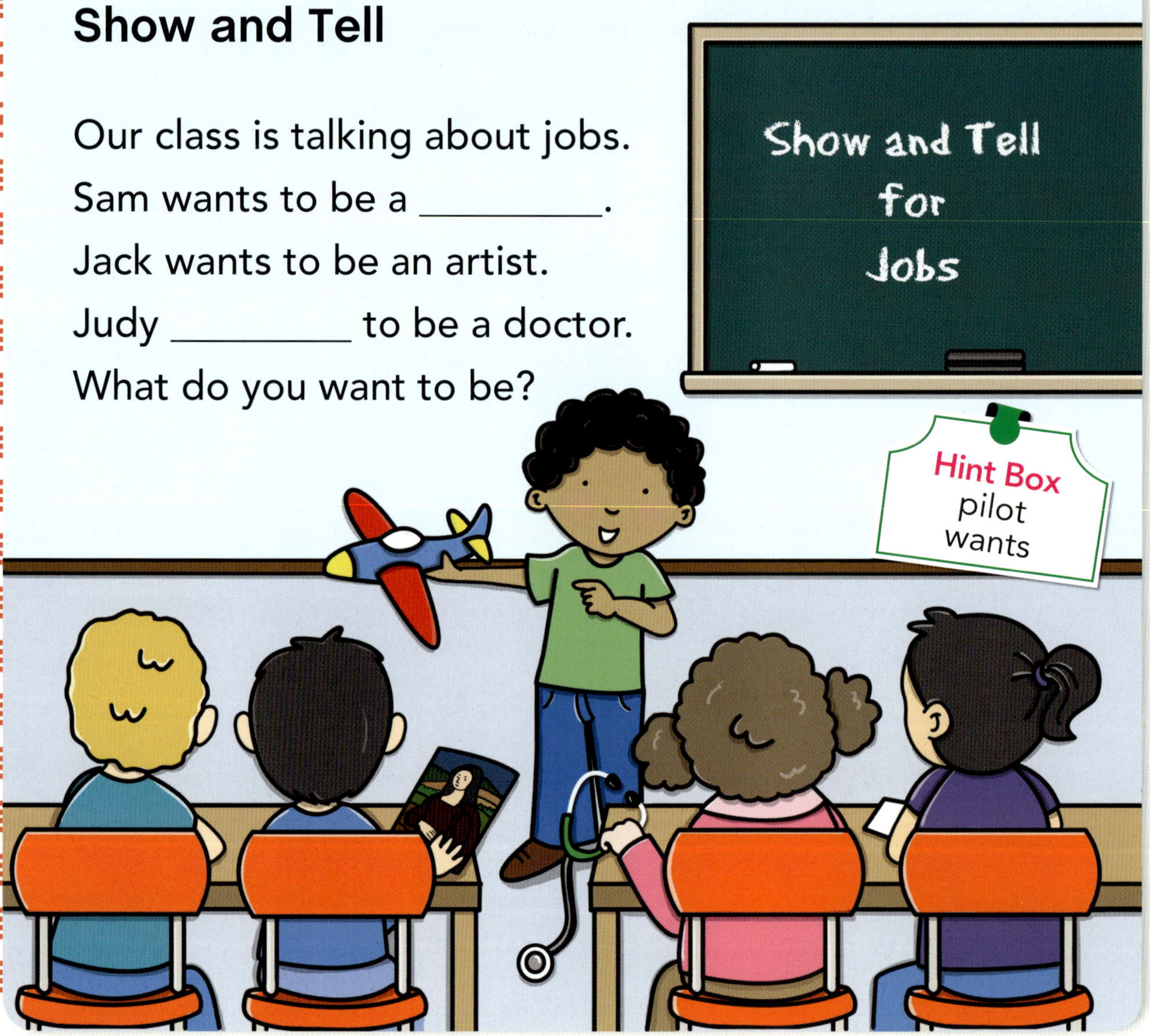

B Read and choose.

1 What are they talking about?

    ⓐ jobs   ⓑ clothes   ⓒ toys

2 What does Judy want to be?

    ⓐ an artist   ⓑ a doctor   ⓒ a pilot

Ask and listen. Then write. 

What to you want to be?

Teacher

I want to be a/an __________________.

Friend 1

I want to be a/an __________________.

Friend 2

I want to be a/an __________________.

Draw your favorite job. Then talk to your class. 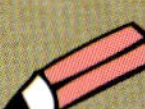

I want to be a/an __________________.

Why Do You Want to Be a Teacher?

Fun Listening

Listen to the cartoon. Then put on the stickers. CD 1 42 / Page 81

Listen, point, and say. CD 1 43

Job ❷

teach kids

help sick people

save people

make food

fly planes

paint pictures

Word Listening

A Listen, match, and say. CD 1 44

1 

2 

- make food -
- save people -
- teach kids -
- paint pictures -
- fly planes -
- help sick people -

3 

4 

5 

6 

B Listen and number. CD 1 45

A **Listen, match, and say.** CD 1 46

1 

• • Because I want to make food.

2 

• • Because I want to save people.

3 

• • Because I want to fly planes.

B **Listen and circle.** CD 1 47

1 

2 

3 

4 

A Listen and repeat. Then practice. (CD 1 48)

B Listen, choose, and write. (CD 1 49)

1.
Q Why do you want to be a doctor?

A Because I want to ______________.

ⓐ help sick people   ⓑ save people   ⓒ make food

2.
Q Why do you want to be a pilot?

A Because I want to ______________.

ⓐ teach kids   ⓑ fly planes   ⓒ paint pictures

C Listen and number. (CD 1 50)

A **Listen and write.** CD 1 51

I Want to Make Food

"Why do you want to be a firefighter?" Jenny asks.

"Because I want to ______________," says Tim.

"Why do you want to be a cook?" Tim asks.

"Because I want to ______________," says Jenny.

"I want to eat your food," says Tim.

B **Read and choose.**

1 What does Tim want to be?

   a a doctor   b a cook   c a firefighter

2 What does Jenny want to do?

   a make food   b paint pictures   c fly planes

Ask and answer. Then write. 

What do you want be? Why?

Down ↓

1. fly _______
2. help _____ people
3. _____ food

Across →

4. _____ kids
5. _____ people
6. paint _____

Draw your dream job. Then talk to your class.

I want to be a/an ____________________.

Because I want to ____________________.

Review Test I

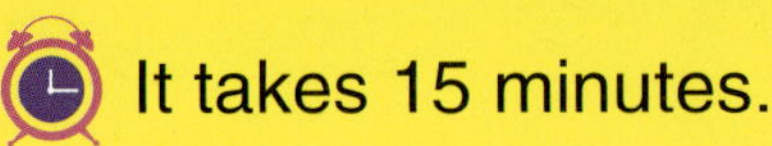 It takes 15 minutes.

Word Check

Listen and circle. (1-4) CD 1 52

1 

2 

3 

4 

Listen and unscramble. (5-8) CD 1 53

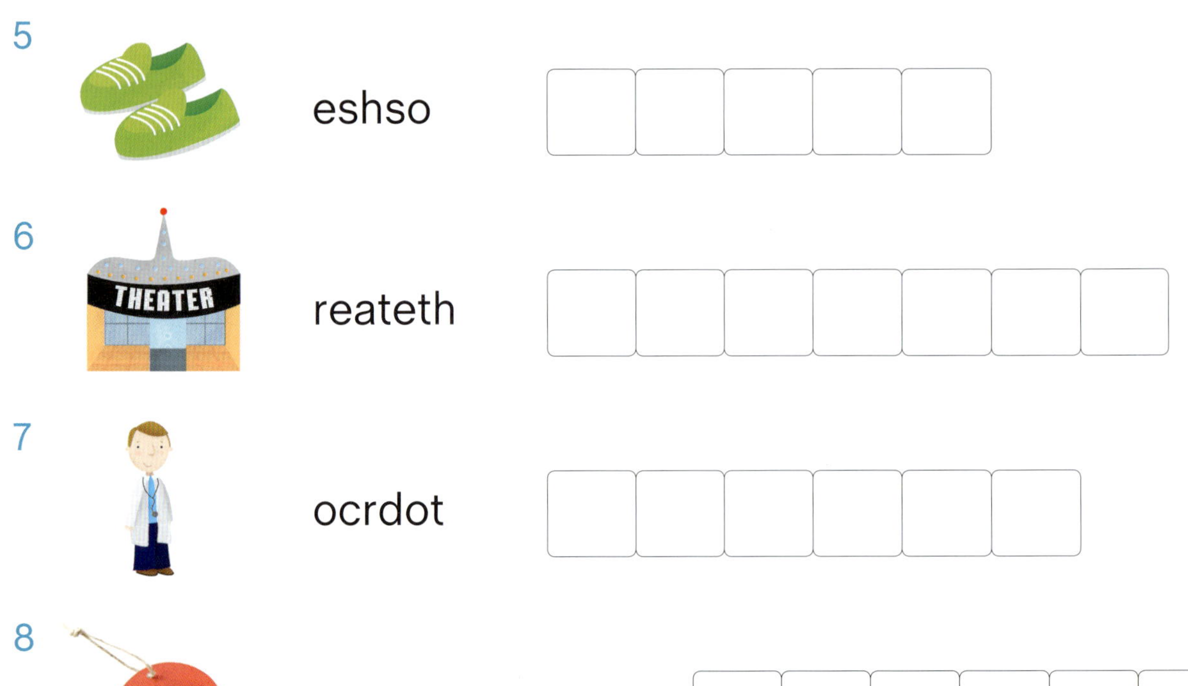

5   eshso

6   reateth

7   ocrdot

8   llarod   one

Listen and circle. (9-11) [CD 1 54]

9

10

11

Listen and choose. (12-16) [CD 1 55]

12 ◯

   a Because I want to make food.

13 ◯

   b It's $1.50.

14 ◯

   c I'm wearing a shirt.

   d I'm going to the pet shop.

15 ◯

   e I want to be a firefighter.

16 ◯

Listen and choose. (17-18) [CD 1 56]

17 **Q** How much is this?

A __________________________

   ⓐ It's $6.40.
   ⓑ I'm wearing a jacket.
   ⓒ I'm going to the mall.

18 **Q** __________________________

A I want to be a teacher.

   ⓐ Where are you going?
   ⓑ What do you want to be?
   ⓒ Why do you want to be a pilot?

Listen and match. (19-21) [CD 1 57]

19

Q Why do you want to be an artist?
A Because I want to paint pictures.

20

Q What are you wearing?
A I'm wearing pants.

21

Q Where are you going?
A I'm going to school.

Listen, circle, and write. (22-26) 🎧 CD 1 58

22

The book is ___________________.

one dollar and fifty cents **I** fifty cents

The doll is ___________________.

one dollar **I** ten dollars

23

The boy is going to the ___________.

park **I** pet shop

The girl is going to the ___________.

mall **I** theater

24

The girl is wearing ___________.

a dress **I** a skirt

The boy is wearing ___________.

a shirt and a jacket **I** pants and shoes

25

The girl wants to be a ___________.

artist **I** teacher

The boy wants to be a ___________.

pilot **I** cook

26

The boy wants to ___________.

make food **I** help sick people

The girl wants to ___________.

paint pictures **I** teach kids

You Can Get There by Train

Fun Listening

Listen to the cartoon. Then put on the stickers. CD 2 02 Page 81

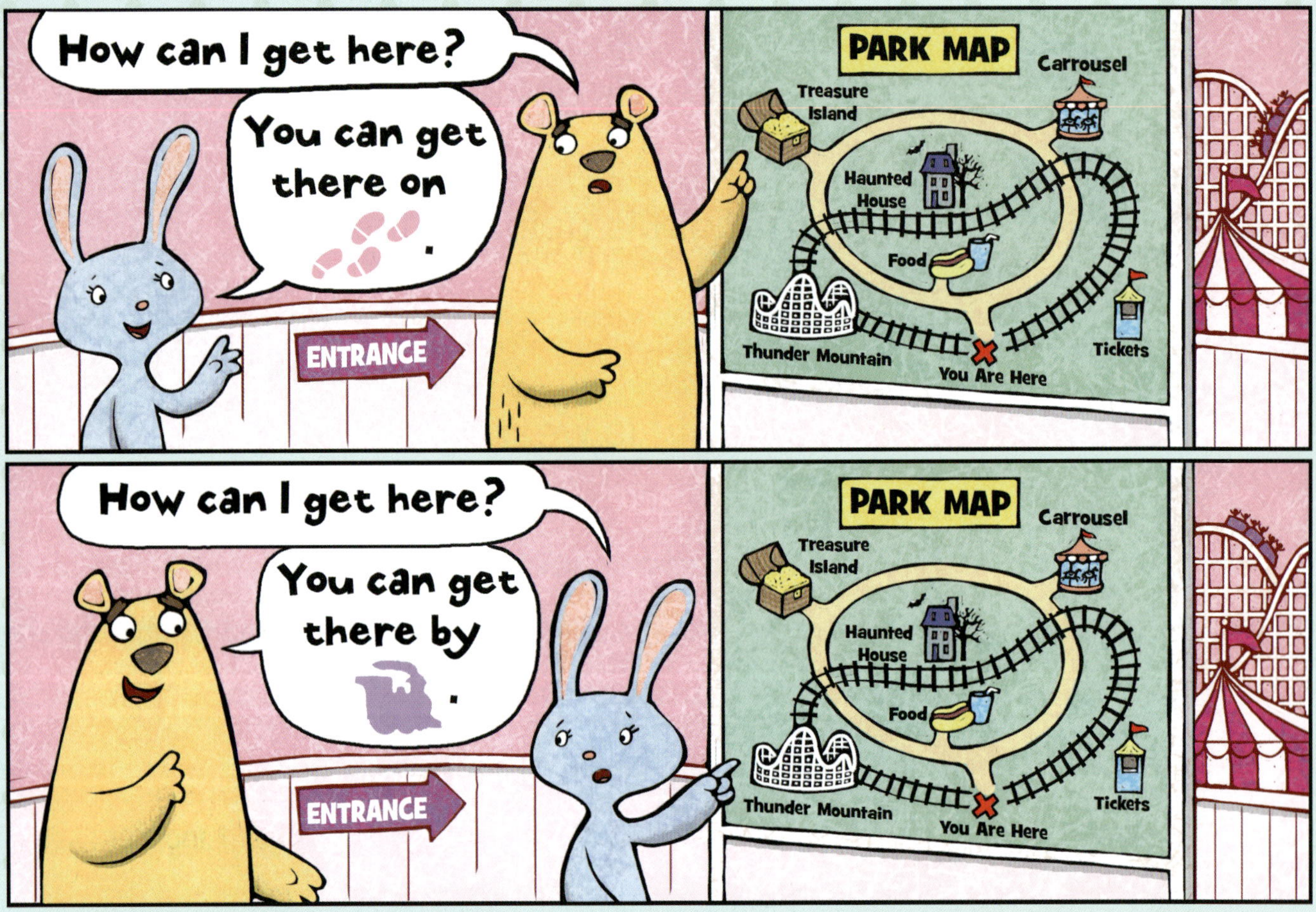

Listen, point, and say. CD 2 03

Transportation

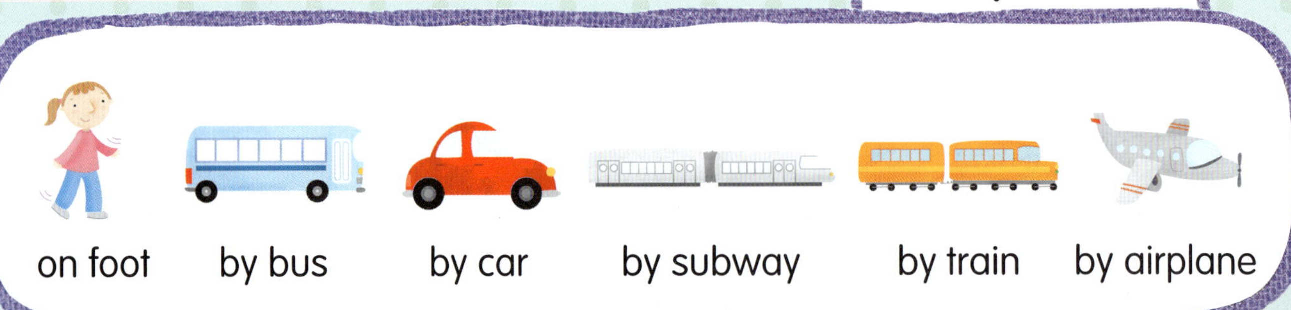

A Listen, match, and say. CD 2 04

1 

2 

- by airplane •
- on foot •
- by bus •
- by subway •
- by car •
- by train

3 

4 

5 

6

B Listen and number. CD 2 05

A Listen, check, and say. CD 2 06

1 

◯ You can get there by bus.

◯ You can get there on foot.

2 

◯ You can get there by train.

◯ You can get there by subway.

3

◯ You can get there by car.

◯ You can get there by airplane.

B Listen and check. CD 2 07

1 

2 

3 

4 

A Listen and repeat. Then practice. 

CD 2 08

B Listen, choose, and write.

CD 2 09

1

Q How can I get there?

A You can get there ________________.

ⓐ by airplane   ⓑ by train   ⓒ by car

2

Q How can I get there?

A You can get there ________________.

ⓐ by bus   ⓑ on foot   ⓒ by subway

C Listen and number.

CD 2 10

Story Listening

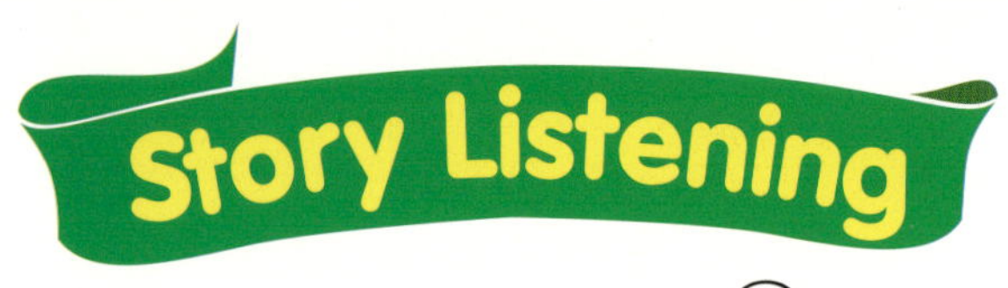

A Listen and write. CD 2 11

How Can I Get There?

Sally wants to go to the zoo.
"How can I ________ there?" she asks.
"You can get there on foot,"
says a policewoman.
"No! It's too far," says a clown.
"You can get there by ________. Let's go!"

Hint Box
get
airplane

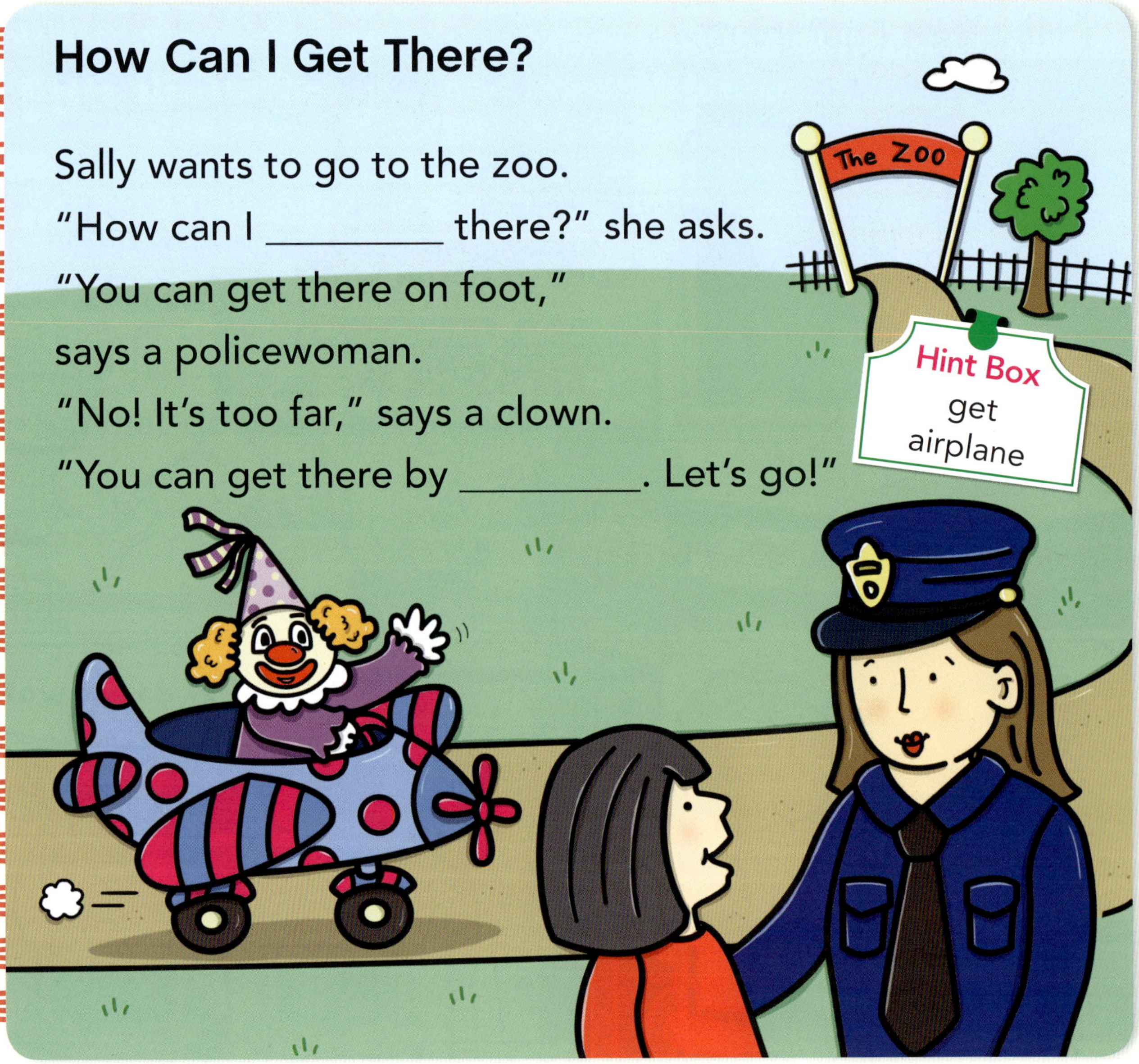

B Read and choose.

1 Where does Sally want to go?

ⓐ to school ⓑ to the zoo ⓒ home

2 How can she get there?

ⓐ by subway ⓑ by bus ⓒ by airplane

Ask and listen. Then write. 

How can I get to the park?

Teacher

You can get to the park _______________.

Friend 1

You can get to the park _______________.

Friend 2

You can get to the park _______________.

Draw how you can get to school. Then talk to your class. 

I can get to school _______________.

I Go Swimming

Listen to the cartoon. Then put on the stickers. CD 2 12 · Page 81

Listen, point, and say. CD 2 13

Seasons & Activities

A Listen, match, and say. (CD 2 14)

1 

2 

3 

4 

5 

6 

- summer
- go skiing
- go swimming
- fall
- go hiking
- winter

B Listen and number. (CD 2 15)

A Listen, match, and say. CD 2 16

1

•

• I go hiking.

2

•

• I go camping.

3

•

• I go swimming.

B Listen and circle. CD 2 17

1

2

3

4

Dialog Listening

A Listen and repeat. Then practice. CD 2 18

B Listen, choose, and write. CD 2 19

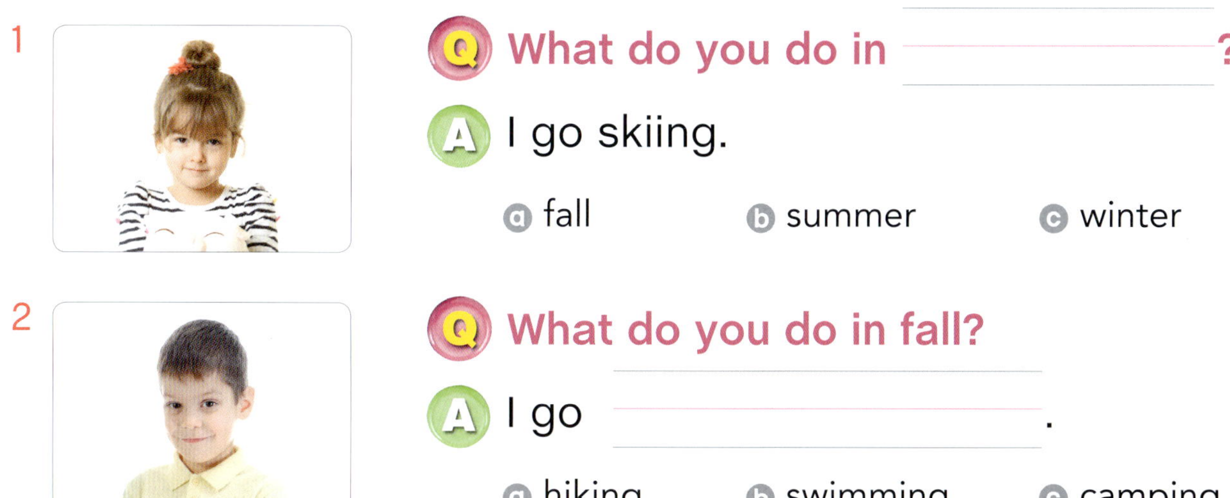

1

Q What do you do in ________________?

A I go skiing.

    a fall   **b** summer   **c** winter

2

Q What do you do in fall?

A I go ________________.

    a hiking   **b** swimming   **c** camping

C Listen and number. CD 2 20

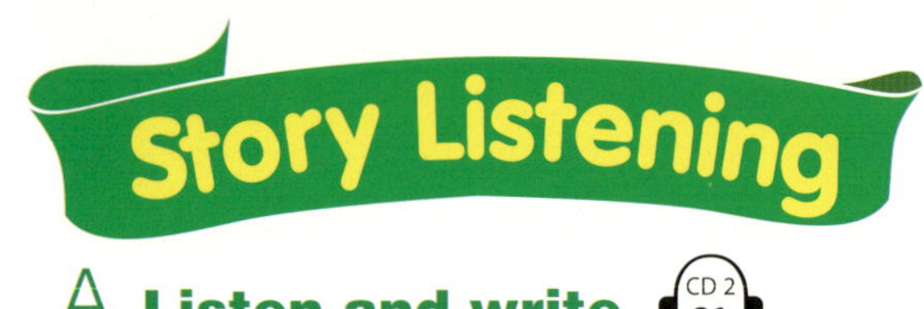

Story Listening

A Listen and write. CD 2 21

In the Summer

Hint Box
Summer
swimming

Jill and Bob go hiking in spring.
__________ is coming soon.
"What do you do in summer?" asks Jill.
"I go __________," says Bob.
"I like swimming. Hiking is hard!"

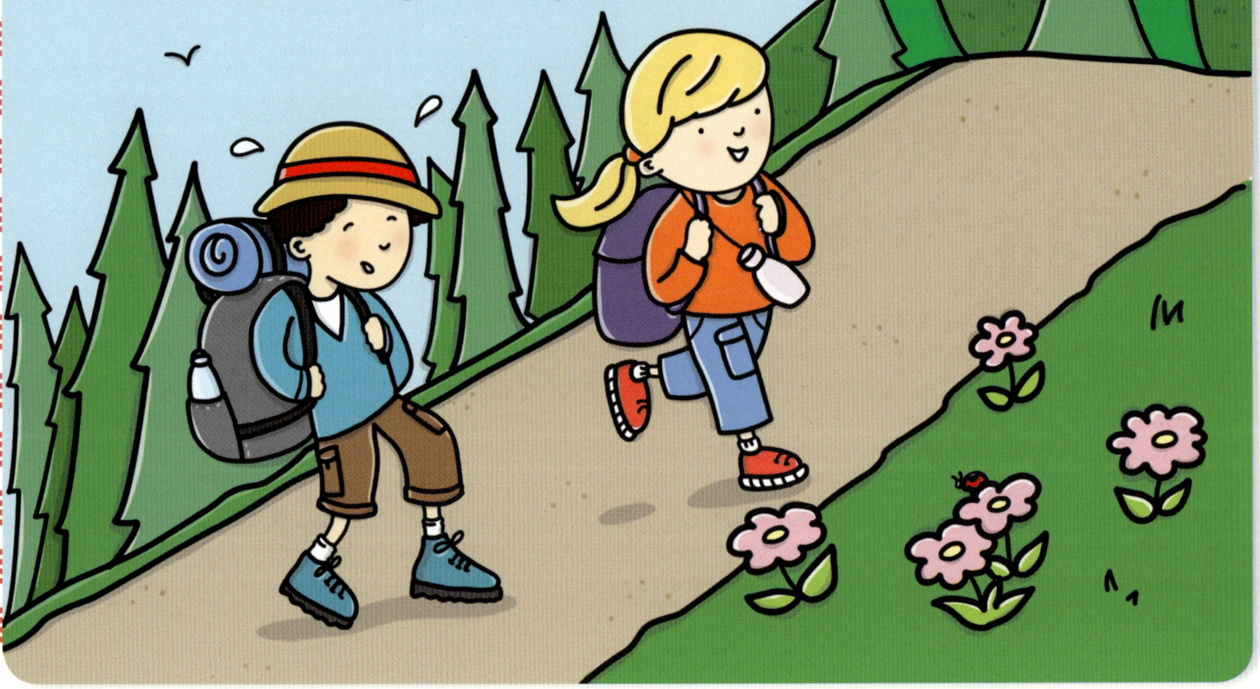

B Read and choose.

1 What season is it?

ⓐ spring ⓑ fall ⓒ winter

2 What does Bob do in summer?

ⓐ go camping ⓑ go swimming ⓒ go skiing

Ask and listen. Then write. 

What do you do in fall?

Teacher

I ____________________ in fall.

Friend 1

I ____________________ in fall.

Friend 2

I ____________________ in fall.

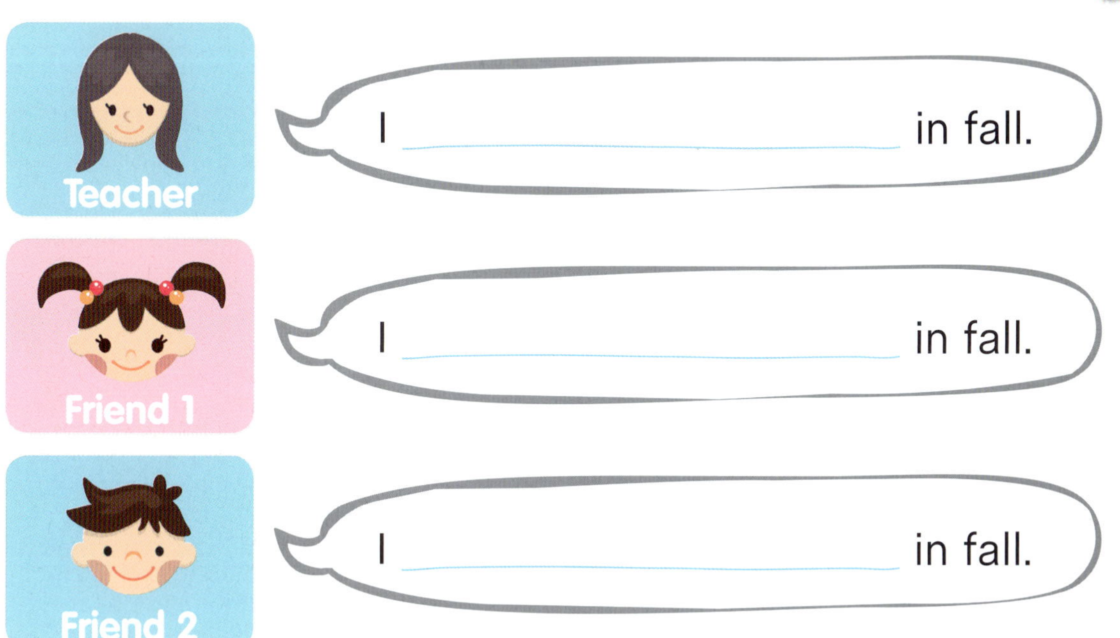

Draw what you do in spring. Then talk to your class.

I ____________________ in spring.

When Is Christmas?

Fun Listening

Listen to the cartoon. Then put on the stickers.  CD 2 22 · Page 81

Listen, point, and say. CD 2 23

Holiday

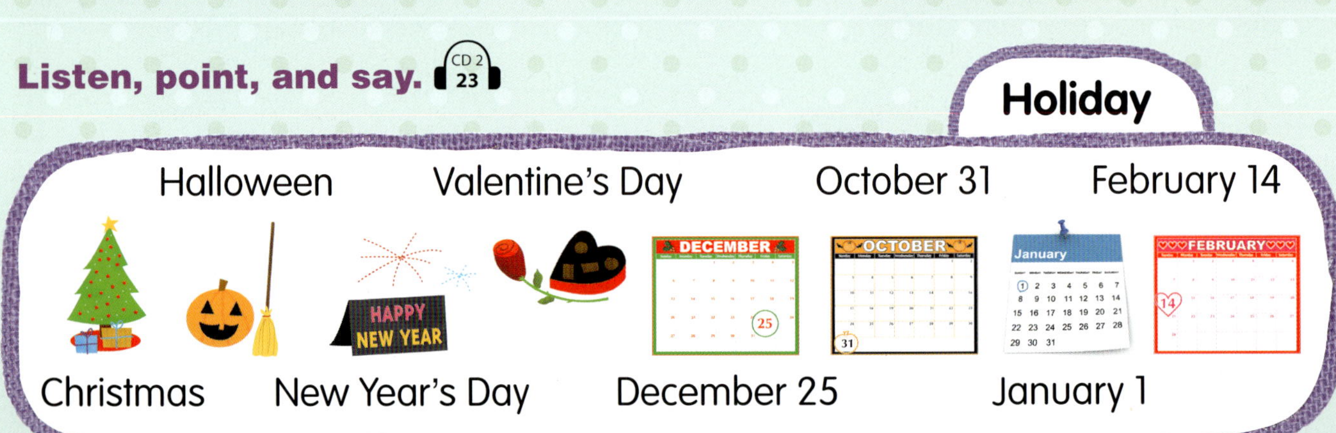

A Listen, circle, and say. CD 2 24

1

Halloween | January 1

2

October 31 | Christmas

3

Valentine's Day | December 25

4

December 25 | Valentine's Day

5

February 14 | New Year's Day

6

Halloween | February 14

B Listen and circle. CD 2 25

1

2

3

4

A Listen, check, and say.  CD 2 26

1

◯ Valentine's Day is on January 1.

◯ Valentine's Day is on February 14.

2

◯ Christmas is on December 25.

◯ Christmas is on December 14.

3

◯ Halloween is on October 31.

◯ Halloween is on February 14.

B Listen and circle. CD 2 27

1

2

3

4

A **Listen and repeat. Then practice.** CD 2 28

B **Listen, choose, and write.** CD 2 29

1 

Q When is New Year's Day?

A New Year's Day is on ___________ .

   ⓐ January 1   ⓑ October 31   ⓒ December 25

2

Q When is ___________ ?

A Halloween is on October 31.

   ⓐ Valentine's Day   ⓑ Christmas   ⓒ Halloween

C **Listen and number.** CD 2 30

A **Listen and write.** CD 2 / 31

When Is Halloween?

Hint Box
Halloween
December 25

"I want to be a vampire," says Tom.

"When is ______________?" asks Tom.

"Halloween is on October 31," answers Jane.

"I want to meet Santa Claus," says Jane.

"Christmas is on ______________," says Tom.

B **Read and choose.**

1 When is Christmas?

  ⓐ January 1　　　ⓑ October 31　　　ⓒ December 25

2 Which holiday is NOT in the story?

  ⓐ Halloween　　　ⓑ New Year's Day　　　ⓒ Christmas

Ask and listen. Then write. 

What is your favorite holiday? When is it? 

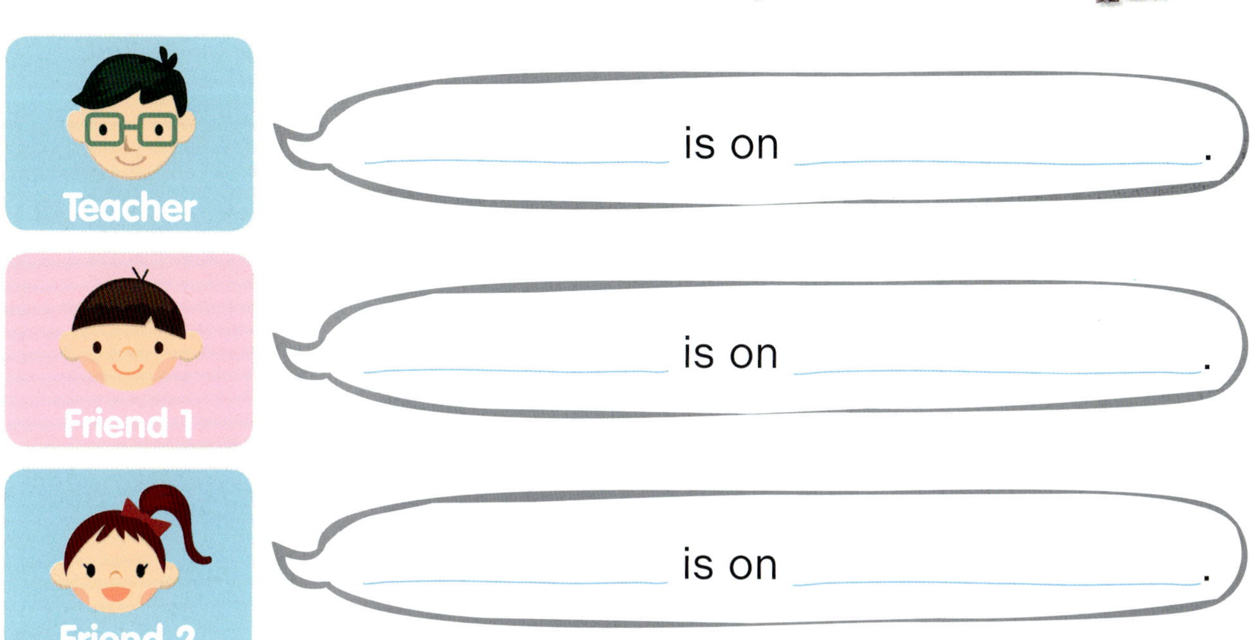

Teacher

___________ is on ___________ .

Friend 1

___________ is on ___________ .

Friend 2

___________ is on ___________ .

Draw your favorite holiday. Then talk to your class.

___________ is on ___________ .

What Is Your Favorite Subject?

Fun Listening

Listen to the cartoon. Then put on the stickers. CD 2 32 · Page 81

Listen, point, and say. CD 2 33

Subject

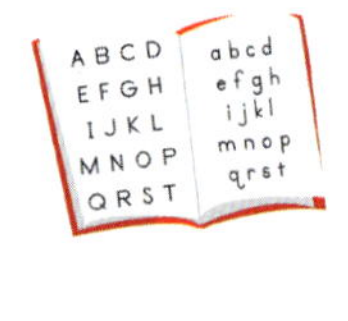

English   science   math   art   music   P.E.

Word Listening

A Listen, match, and say. (CD 2 - 34)

1 

2

- art
- English
- math
- music
- science
- P.E.

3 

4

5 

6

B Listen and number. (CD 2 - 35)

A Listen, match, and say. CD 2 36

1

2

3

• My favorite subject is art.

• My favorite subject is science

• My favorite subject is P.E.

B Listen and circle. CD 2 37

1

2

3

4

A Listen and repeat. Then practice. CD 2 38

B Listen, choose, and write. CD 2 39

1

Q What is your favorite subject?

A My favorite subject is _______.

ⓐ music   ⓑ art   ⓒ science

2

Q What is your favorite subject?

A My favorite subject is _______.

ⓐ math   ⓑ English   ⓒ P.E.

C Listen and number. CD 2 40

Story Listening

A Listen and write. CD 2 41

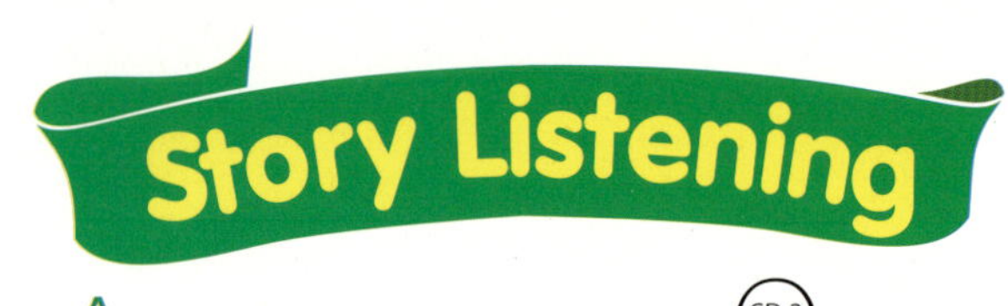

My Favorite Subject

Hint Box
P.E.
English

Sam and Julie are excited to start school.
"What is your favorite subject?" asks Sam.
"My favorite subject is __________," says Julie.
"What is your favorite subject?" asks Julie.
"My favorite subject is __________,"
says Sam.

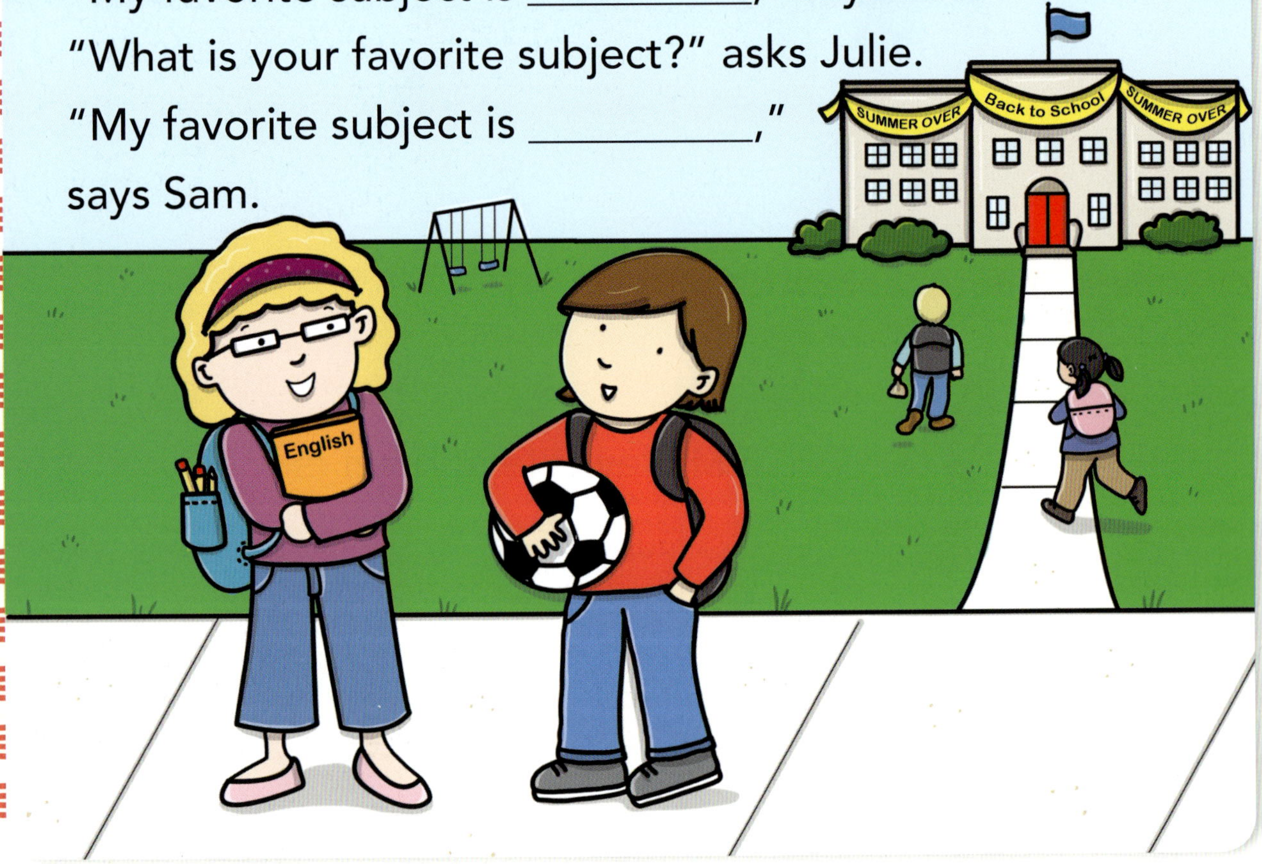

B Read and choose.

1 Who likes English?

ⓐ Sam ⓑ Julie ⓒ Sam and Julie

2 What is Sam's favorite subject?

ⓐ P.E. ⓑ English ⓒ math

Ask and listen. Then write. 

What is your favorite subject?

Teacher

My favorite subject is __________.

Friend 1

My favorite subject is __________.

Friend 2

My favorite subject is __________.

Draw your favorite subject. Then talk to your class. 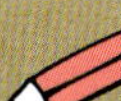

My favorite subject is __________.

Sit Down, Please

Fun Listening

Listen to the cartoon. Then put on the stickers.  CD 2 42 Page 81

Listen, point, and say. CD 2 43

School Rules

A Listen, match, and say. CD 2 44

1 

2 

run

quiet

fight

stand

late

sit

3 

4  

5 

6 

B Listen and circle. CD 2 45

1  

2

3  

4

A Listen, match, and say. CD 2 46

1 

2 

3 

- Okay, I won't run.

- Okay, I will stand up.

- Okay, I will sit down.

B Listen and check. CD 2 47

1 

2 

3 

4 

Dialog Listening

A **Listen and repeat. Then practice.** CD 2 48

B **Listen, choose, and write.** CD 2 49

1

A Don't run.

B Okay, I _________________ .

ⓐ will be quiet   ⓑ won't run   ⓒ won't fight.

2

A _________________ , please.

B Okay, I will stand up.

ⓐ stand up   ⓑ sit down   ⓒ be late

C **Listen and number.** CD 2 50

Story Listening

A **Listen and write.** (CD 2 51)

In the Library

Peter is playing in the library.

"Be _________, please!" says the librarian.

"Don't run! Sit down!" she says.

"Okay, I will be quiet," Peter says.

"I won't run. I will _________ down."

B **Read and choose.**

1 Where is Peter playing?

    (a) in a library   (b) on a bus   (c) at a swimming pool

2 What will Peter do?

    (a) He won't fight.   (b) He will be late.   (c) He will sit down.

Look and say. Then write. 

Don't ___________ . / ___________ , please.

Down ⬇

❶ Don't ______

❷ ______ down

❸ Don't ______

Across ➡

❹ ______ up

❺ Be ______

❻ Don't be ______

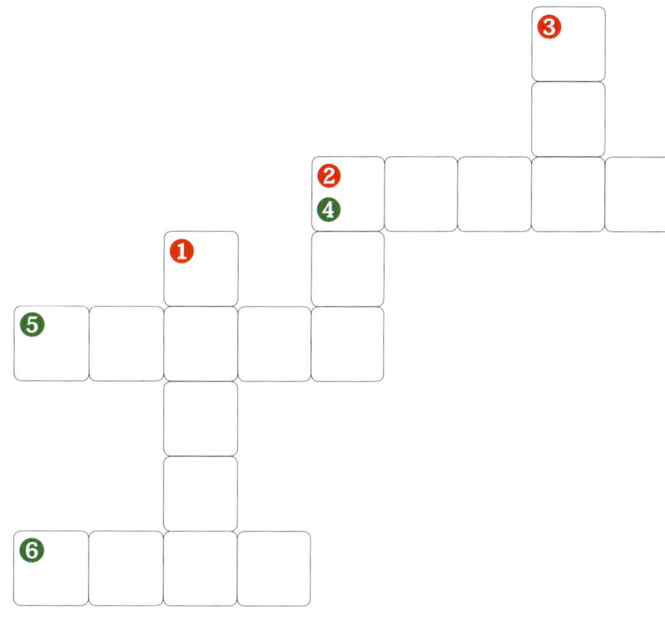

Draw one thing you should do. Then talk to your class. ✏

Okay, I ___________________ .

Review Test II 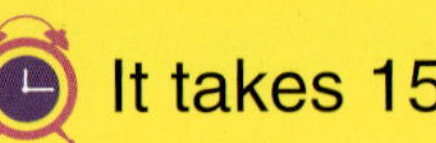 It takes 15 minutes.

Total Score
/ 26

Listen and circle. (1-4) CD 2 52

1
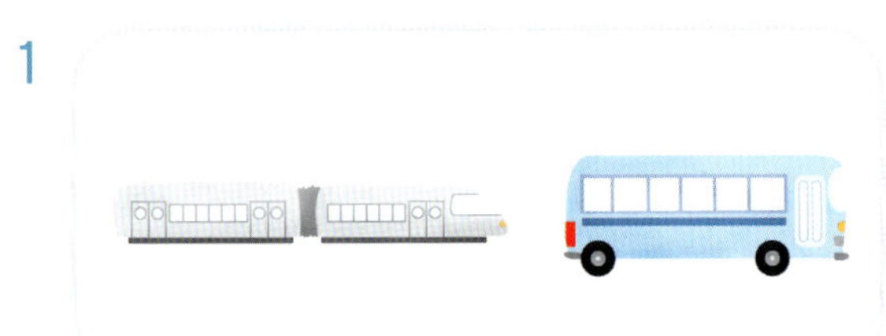

2

3

4

Listen and unscramble. (5-8) CD 2 53

5

ristChmas

6

msmeru

7

eceiscn

8

anrti

by

Listen and circle. (9-11) CD 2 54

9   

10   

11   

Listen and choose. (12-16) CD 2 55

12 ◯

13 ◯

14 ◯

15 ◯

16 ◯

    a I go swimming.

    b Okay, I won't be late.

    c New Year's Day is on January 1.

    d You can get there by subway.

    e My favorite subject is music.

Listen and choose. (17-18) (CD 2 56)

17 Q What do you do in spring?

A _______________________________

- ⓐ I go hiking.
- ⓑ Halloween is on October 31.
- ⓒ You can get there by bus.

18 Q _______________________________

A My favorite subject is math.

- ⓐ What do you do in fall?
- ⓑ When is New Year's Day?
- ⓒ What is your favorite subject?

Listen and match. (19-21) (CD 2 57)

19 

20 

21 

Q How can I get there?
A You can get there by airplane.

A Be quiet, please.
B Okay, I will be quiet.

Q When is Valentine's Day?
A Valentine's Day is on February 14.

Listen, circle, and write. (22-26) 🎧 CD 2 58

22 

Christmas is on ___________________ .

December 25 | January 1

Halloween is on ___________________ .

February 14 | October 31

23 

His favorite subject is ___________________ .

music | P.E.

Her favorite subject is ___________________ .

science | math

24 

She won't ___________________ .

fight | run

She will ___________________ .

sit down | be quiet

25 

He goes ___________________ in spring.

hiking | camping

She goes swimming in ___________________ .

winter | summer

26 

He can get there by ___________________ .

subway | car

She can get there by ___________________ .

airplane | bus

Word List

 Clothes

shirt

pants

skirt

jacket

dress

shoes

 Price

twenty-five cents

fifty cents

one dollar

one dollar and fifty cents

six dollars and forty cents

ten dollars

 # Place

theater

school

bank

mall

park

pet shop

 # Job ❶

firefighter

doctor

teacher

cook

pilot

artist

 # Job ❷

teach kids

help sick people

save people

make food

fly planes

paint pictures

Unit 06 Transportation

   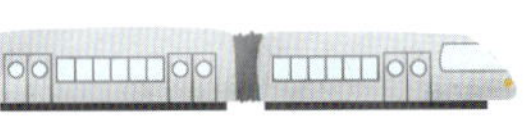  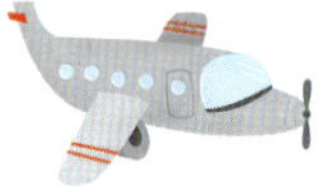

| on foot | by bus | by car | by subway | by train | by airplane |

Unit 07 Seasons & Activities

| spring | summer | fall | winter |

| go hiking | go swimming | go camping | go skiing |

Unit 08 Holiday

| Christmas | Halloween | New Year's Day | Valentine's Day |

| December 25 | October 31 | January 1 | February 14 |

Subject

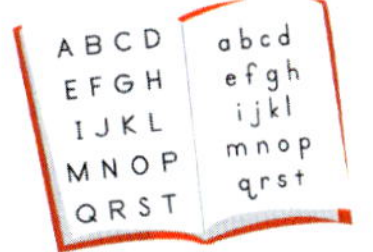

English

science

math

art

music

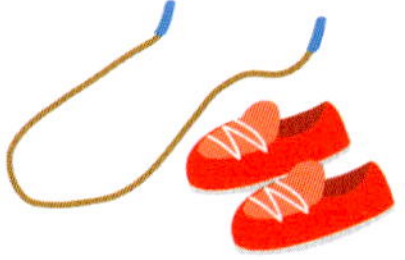

P.E.

School Rules

sit

quiet

stand

run

fight

late

I Meet Listening 3

Written by Brian Stuart
Illustrated by Jennifer Morris·Holli Conger·Roz Fulcher

First Published November 2012
Fifth Printing November 2020

Publisher: Kyudo Chung
Editorial Manager: Mija Cho
Editors: Genie Jeong, Mikyoung Kim, Jungwon Min
Designers: Eunhee Lee, Soonam Park
Cover Design: Eunhee Lee, Soonam Park

Published and distributed by Happy House, an imprint of DARAKWON
Darakwon Bldg., 211 Moonbal-ro, Paju-si Gyeonggi-do, Korea 10881
Tel: 82-2-736-2031(Ext. 250) **Fax:** 82-2-732-2037 **Homepage:** www.ihappyhouse.co.kr

ISBN: 978-89-6653-090-8 68740
Age Range: 7 years and up
Price: ₩13,000

[Components]
• Student Book
• Workbook
• 2 Audio CDs
(Answer Key / Audio Script / MP3 Files / Word Test: free download at **www.ihappyhouse.co.kr**)

Stickers

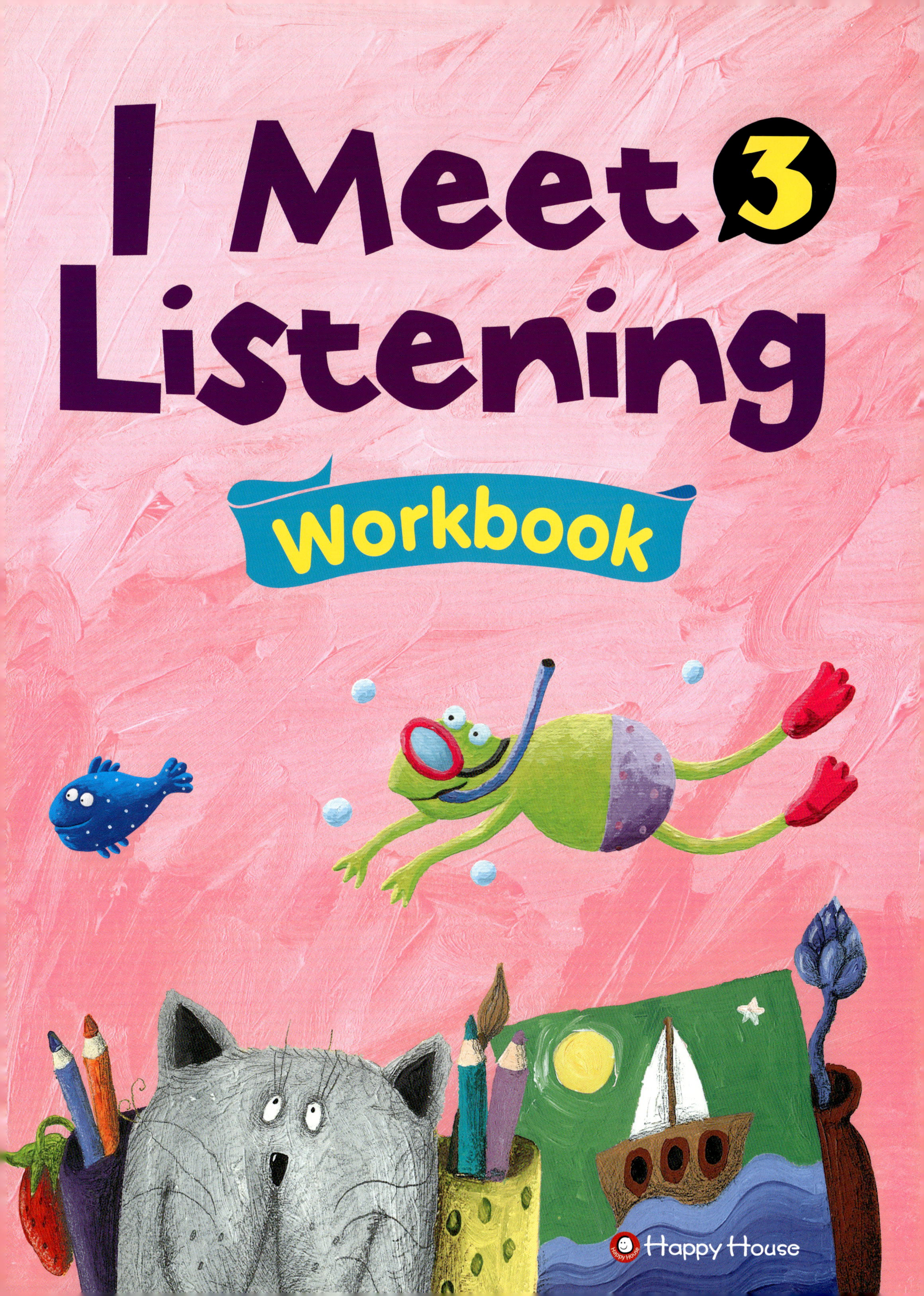
I Meet
3
Listening
Workbook
Happy House

Written by Brian Stuart
Illustrated by Jennifer Morris·Holli Conger·Roz Fulcher

Publisher: Kyudo Chung
Editorial Manager: Mija Cho
Editors: Genie Jeong, Mikyoung Kim, Jungwon Min
Designers: Eunhee Lee, Soonam Park
Cover Design: Eunhee Lee, Soonam Park

Published and distributed by Happy House, an imprint of DARAKWON
Darakwon Bldg., 211 Moonbal-ro, Paju-si Gyeonggi-do, Korea 10881
Tel: 82-2-736-2031(Ext. 250) **Fax:** 82-2-732-2037 **Homepage:** www.ihappyhouse.co.kr

ISBN: 978-89-6653-090-8 68740
Age Range: 7 years and up

I Meet Listening 3

Workbook

CONTENTS

What Are You Wearing?

Word Practice

A Look, write, and say.

1 
dress

2 
pants

3 
skirt

4 
jacket

5 
shirt

6 
shoes

B Listen and check. CD 1 59

1 
 a
 b

2 
 a
b

3 
 a
b

4 
 a
 b

Listen and unscramble. CD 1 60

1  a / I'm / jacket / wearing / .

2  you / are / What / wearing / ?

3  shoes / I'm / wearing / .

Listen and write. CD 1 61

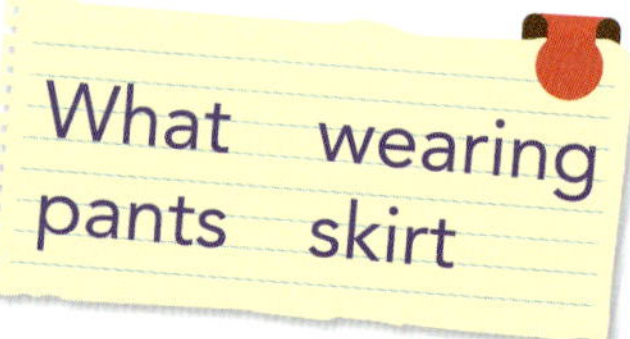

1 

Q What are you _______?

A I'm wearing _______.

2 

Q _______ are you wearing?

A I'm wearing a _______.

Story Practice

A **Listen and write.** (CD 1 62)

It's Time for a Play!

They have a play today.

Mark is ___________ a big ___________.

Nancy is wearing a ___________ and shoes.

Jim is wearing a shirt and ___________.

They ___________ great!

> **Hint Box**
> pants   jacket   look   wearing   dress

B **Read and check.**

1 It's time for a movie. ⊙ ☐   ✗ ☐

2 Nancy is wearing shoes. ⊙ ☐   ✗ ☐

3 Jim is wearing a skirt. ⊙ ☐   ✗ ☐

How Much Is This?

Word Practice

A **Look, write, and say.**

1 $ 1.50
one dollar and
fifty cents

2 $ 10.00
ten dollars

3 $ 1.00
one dollar

4 $ 6.40
six dollars and
forty cents

5 25 ¢
twenty-five cents

6 50 ¢
fifty cents

B **Listen and check.** CD 1 63

1 

a
b

2

a
b

3 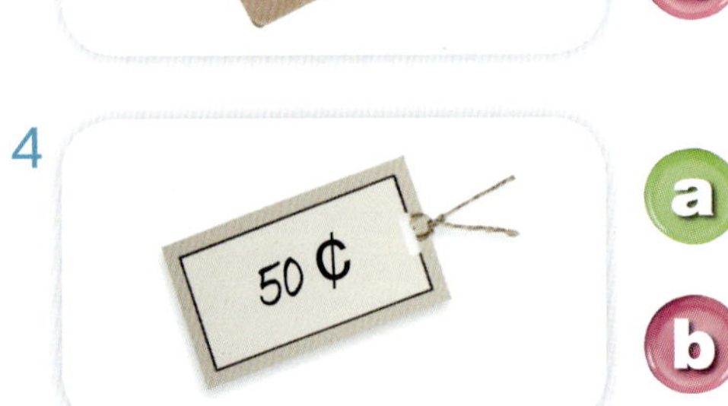

a
b

4

a
b

Listen and unscramble. CD 1 64

1  dollar / one / It's / .

____

2  much / is / this / How / ?

____

3  and / forty cents / It's / six dollars / .

____

Listen and write. CD 1 65

1 

Q How _____________ is this?

A It's ten _____________.

2 

Q _____________ much is this?

A It's one dollar and fifty _____________.

A Listen and write. (CD 1 / 66)

John Can't Buy It

Jane asks, "__________ much is this cup?"

The woman says, "__________ $1.50."

John asks, "How __________ is this T-shirt?"

The woman says, "It's __________."

John only has $5. He can't __________ it.

> **Hint Box**
> buy $6.40   much   How   It's

B Read and check.

1 John wants to buy shoes.  

2 The T-shirt is $6.40.  

3 John only has $1.50.   

I'm Going to the Park

Word Practice

A Look, write, and say.

1 
park
____

2 
bank
____

3 
school
____

4 
mall
____

5 
pet shop
____

6 
theater
____

B Listen and check. CD 1 67

1 
a
b

2 
a
b

3 
a
b

4 
a
b

Listen and unscramble. CD 1 68

1  to / the / I'm / park / going / .

2  going / you / are / Where / ?

3  pet shop / the / going / to / I'm / .

Listen and write. CD 1 69

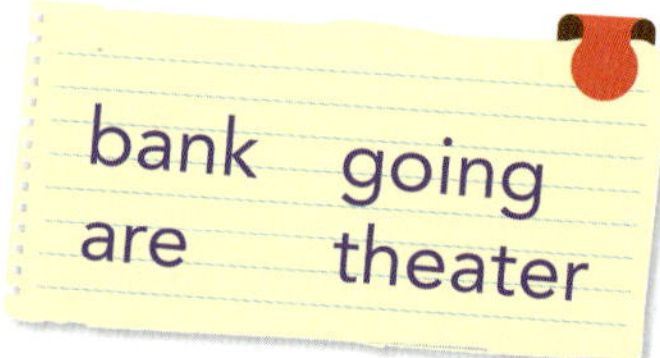

1 

Q Where are you ___________?

A I'm going to the ___________.

2

Q Where ___________ you going?

A I'm going to the ___________.

A **Listen and write.** CD 1 / 70

Where Are You Going?

Linda meets Tom and Kate

in the ___________.

Tom is ___________ to school.

Kate is going to the ___________.

"___________ are you going, Linda?" they ask.

"Oops! I'm going to the ___________!" says Linda.

Hint Box

Where   pet shop   park   theater   going

B **Read and check.**

1 They are in the park.   ⊙ ☐   ✖ ☐

2 Kate is going to school.   ⊙ ☐   ✖ ☐

3 Linda is going to the pet shop.   ⊙ ☐   ✖ ☐

I Want to Be a Teacher

Word Practice

A Look, write, and say.

1 
firefighter

2 
doctor

3 
teacher

4 
pilot

5 
artist

6 
cook

B Listen and check. CD 1 71

1  a b

2  a b

3 a b

4 a b

Listen and unscramble. CD 1 72

1 an / I / artist / be / want / to / .

2 be / do / you / What / want / to / ?

3 a / teacher / I / want / be / to / .

Listen and write. CD 1 73

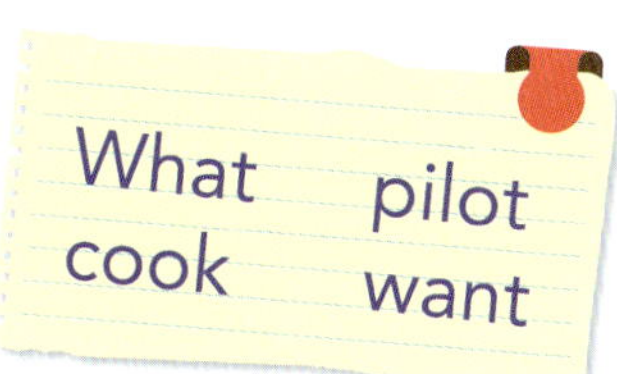

1 **Q** What do you __________ to be?

   A I want to be a __________ .

2 **Q** __________ do you want to be?

   A I want to be a __________ .

A Listen and write. (CD 1 / 74)

Show and Tell

Our class is talking about __________.

Sam __________ to be a pilot.

Jack wants to be an __________.

Judy wants to be a __________.

What do __________ want to be?

Show and Tell

Hint Box

you   jobs   wants   doctor   artist

B Read and check.

1 Our class is talking about places.   O ☐   X ☐

2 Jack wants to be an artist.   O ☐   X ☐

3 Judy wants to be a pilot.   O ☐   X ☐

Unit 05 — Why Do You Want to Be a Teacher?

Word Practice

A Look, write, and say.

1 
help sick people

2 
make food

3 
fly planes

4 
paint pictures

5 
teach kids

6 
save people

B Listen and check. CD 1 75

1 
 a
 b

2 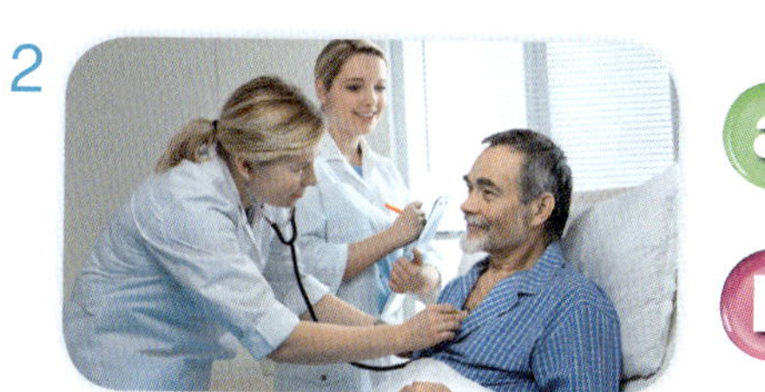
a
b

3 
 a
 b

4 
 a
 b

Listen and unscramble. CD 1 76

1  teach / want / kids / Because / I / to / .

2  do / want / a pilot / you / Why / to / be / ?

3  I / to / help / Because / want / sick people / .

Listen and write. CD 1 77

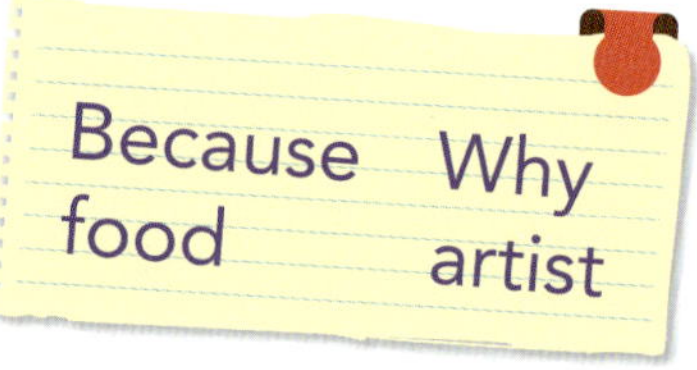

1 

Q __________ do you want to be a cook?

A Because I want to make __________ .

2 

Q Why do you want to be an __________ ?

A __________ I want to paint pictures.

A Listen and write. CD 1 78

I Want to Make Food

"Why do you want to be a ____________?"

Jenny asks.

"Because I want to ____________ people," says Tim.

"____________ do you want to be a ____________?" Tim asks.

"Because I want to make ____________," says Jenny.

"I want to eat your food," says Tim.

Hint Box

firefighter   food   cook   Why   save

B Read and check.

1 Jenny wants to be an artist.

2 Tim wants to save people.

3 Tim wants to eat Jenny's food.

You Can Get There by Train

Word Practice

A **Look, write, and say.**

1 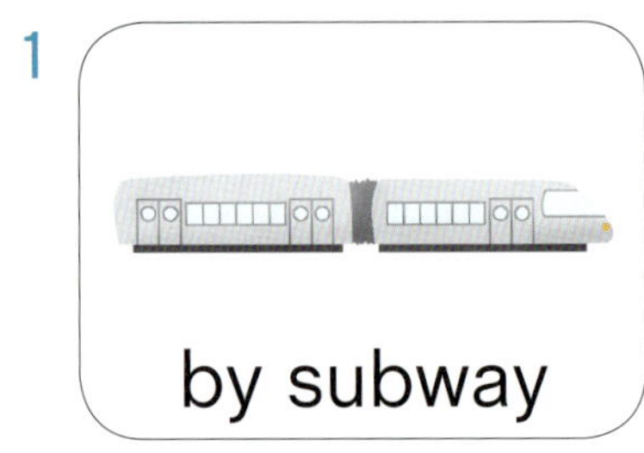
by subway

2 
by car

3 
by train

4 
by bus

5 
on foot

6 
by airplane

B **Listen and check.** CD 2 59

1  **a** **b**

2  **a** **b**

3  **a** **b**

4  **a** **b**

Listen and unscramble. (CD 2 60)

1  on / can / get / You / there / foot / .

2  get / How / I / there / can / ?

3  train / can / You / there / by / get / .

Listen and write. (CD 2 61)

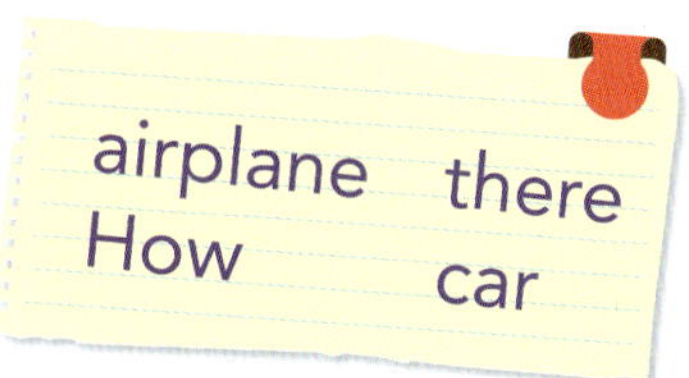

1 
Q ___________ can I get there?

A You can get there by ___________ .

2 
Q How can I get ___________ ?

A You can get there by ___________ .

A **Listen and write.** CD 2 / 62

How Can I Get There?

Sally wants to go to the zoo.

"How can I get __________?" she asks.

"You __________ get there on __________,"

says a policewoman.

"No! It's too far," says a clown.

"You can __________ there __________ airplane. Let's go!"

> **Hint Box**
> foot　　by　　get　　there　　can

B **Read and check.**

1 Sally wants to go to the zoo.　　O ☐　　X ☐

2 Sally can get there by bus.　　O ☐　　X ☐

3 The zoo is not far.　　O ☐　　X ☐

I Go Swimming

Word Practice

A Look, write, and say.

1 
summer

2 
go skiing

3 
winter

4 
go swimming

5 
fall

6 
go hiking

B Listen and check. CD 2 63

1   a  b

2  a b

3   a  b

4  a b

Listen and unscramble. CD 2 64

1  swimming / I / go / .

2  in / do / you / do / What / fall / ?

3  go / skiing / I / .

Listen and write. CD 2 65

1  Q What do you do in _______?

A I go _______.

2  Q _______ do you do in fall?

A I _______ camping.

A Listen and write.

In the Summer

Jill and Bob go hiking in __________.

Summer is coming soon.

"What do you do __________ __________?" asks Jill.

"I __________ swimming," says Bob.

"I like swimming. __________ is hard!"

Hint Box

spring   Hiking   summer   go   in

B Read and check.

1 Jill and Bob go camping.   O ☐   X ☐

2 Bob goes swimming in summer.   O ☐   X ☐

3 Bob likes hiking.   O ☐   X ☐

When Is Christmas?

Word Practice

A Look, write, and say.

1 
Halloween

2 
December 25

3 
Valentine's Day

4 
February 14

5 
Christmas

6 
October 31

B Listen and check. CD 2 67

1 
a
b

2 
a
b

3
a
b

4
a
b

Sentence Practice

Listen and unscramble. CD 2 68

1  Halloween / October / is / 31 / on / .

2  When / Day / Year's / New / is / ?

3  14 / is / on / February / Valentine's Day / .

Dialog Practice

Listen and write. CD 2 69

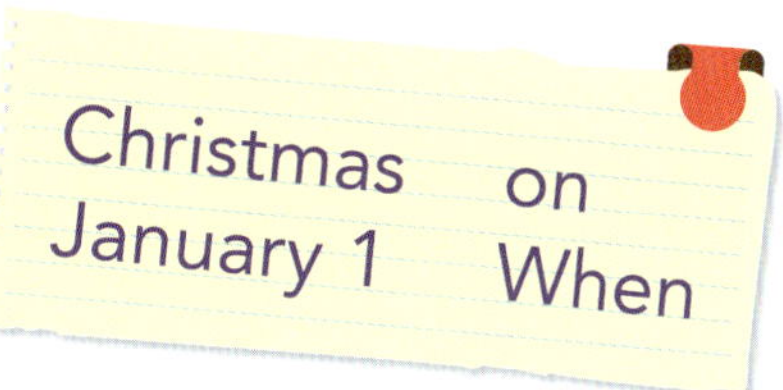

1 

Q When is ________________?

A Christmas is ________ December 25.

2 

Q ________ is New Year's Day?

A New Year's Day is on ________ .

A Listen and write. CD 2 70

When Is Halloween?

"I want to be a vampire," says Tom.

"__________ is Halloween?" asks Tom.

"__________ is on __________ 31," answers Jane.

"I want to meet Santa Claus," says Jane.

"__________ is on __________ 25," says Tom.

> **Hint Box**
> Halloween   December   When   October   Christmas

B Read and check.

1 Halloween is on February 14.  

2 Tom wants to meet Santa Claus.  

3 Christmas is on December 25.   

Unit 09 — What Is Your Favorite Subject?

Word Practice

A Look, write, and say.

1

science

2

art

3
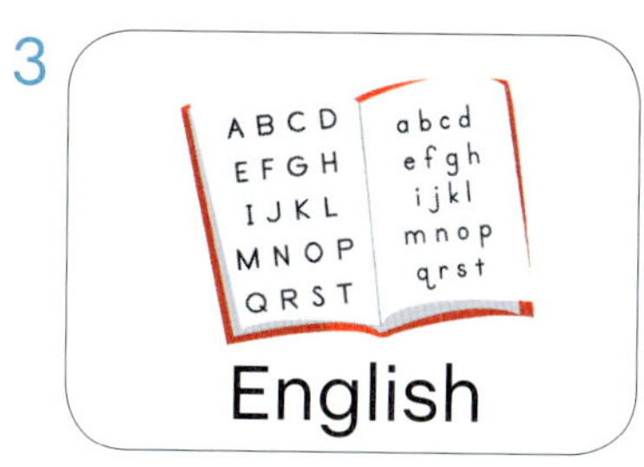
English

4
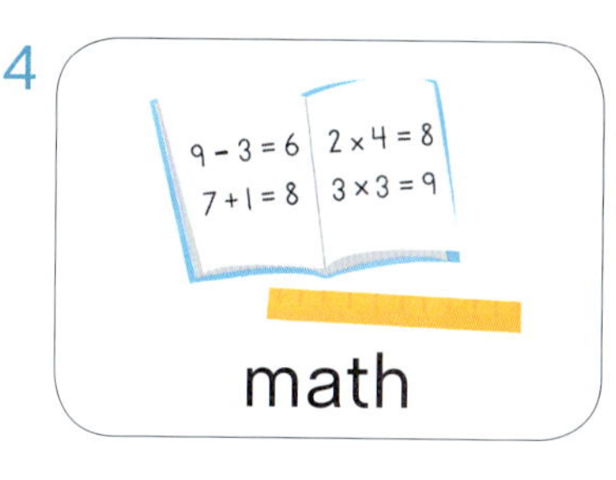
math

5
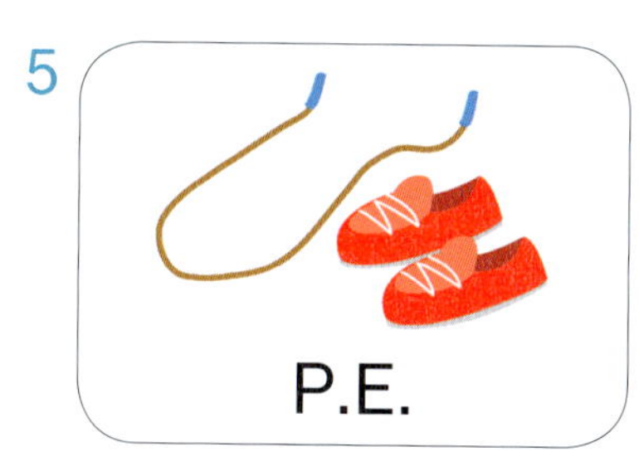
P.E.

6

music

B Listen and check. CD 2 71

1

a
b

2
a
b

3
a
b

4

a
b

Sentence Practice

Listen and unscramble. CD 2 72

1      favorite / art / My / is / subject / .

2      your / is / subject / What / favorite / ?

3      subject / favorite / is / My / math / .

Dialog Practice

Listen and write. CD 2 73

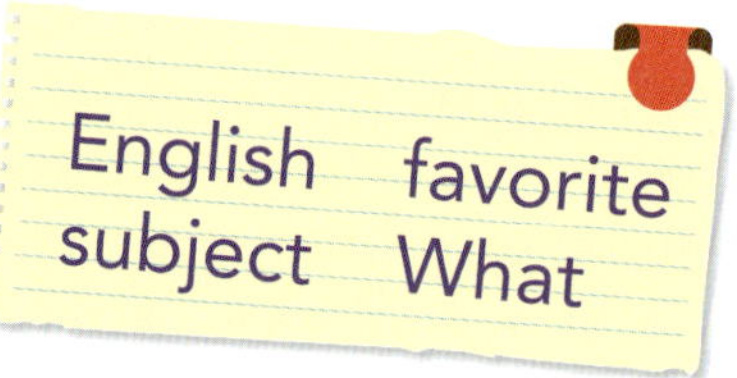

1   

Q What is your favorite ______________?

A My ______________ subject is music.

2   

Q ______________ is your favorite subject?

A My favorite subject is ______________.

A Listen and write. CD 2 / 74

My Favorite Subject

Sam and Julie are excited to start school.

"What is __________ favorite subject?" asks Sam.

"My favorite __________ is English," says Julie.

"__________ is your favorite subject?" asks Julie.

"My __________ subject is __________," says Sam.

> **Hint Box**
> What   P.E.   favorite   subject   your

B Read and check.

1 Sam and Julie like school.  

2 Julie's favorite subject is English.  

3 Sam's favorite subject is math.   

10 Sit Down, Please

Word Practice

A Look, write, and say.

1 
run

___

2 
quiet

___

3 
stand

___

4 
late

___

5 
fight

___

6 
sit

___

B Listen and check. CD 2 / 75

1 
a
b

2
a
b

3
a
b

4 
a
b

Listen and unscramble.  CD 2 76

1. 

   won't / Okay / run / , / I / .

2. 

   up / Stand / please / , / .

3. 

   be / I / quiet / Okay / , / will / .

Listen and write. CD 2 77

1. 

   A Sit down, _____________ .

   B Okay, I will _____________ down.

2. 

   A Don't _____________ .

   B Okay, I _____________ fight.

A **Listen and write.** CD 2 78

In the Library

Peter is playing in the library.

"Be ____________, please!" says the librarian.

"Don't ____________! ____________ down!" she says.

"Okay, I ____________ be quiet," Peter says.

"I ____________ run. I will sit down."

> **Hint Box**
> quiet   will   run   Sit   won't

In the Library

B **Read and check.**

1 Peter is quiet.     

2 Peter will sit down.    

3 Peter won't run.      

I Meet Listening Series
I Meet Listening ❶
I Meet Listening ❷
I Meet Listening ❸